RIDING LIONS

RIDING LIONS

A Journey Through Wind, Wilderness, and the Untamed Soul

L. Seth Burchill

©2025 All Rights Reserved. No portion of this book may be reproduced, stored in a retrieval system, or transmitted in any form or by any means—electronic, mechanical, photocopy, recording, scanning, or other—except for brief quotations in critical reviews or articles without the prior permission of the author.

Published by Game Changer Publishing

Paperback ISBN: 978-1-968250-53-9

Hardcover ISBN: 978-1-968250-54-6

Digital ISBN: 978-1-968250-55-3

www.GameChangerPublishing.com

This book is dedicated to my daughter, Gwendolyn Mae.

"Choose to love God, love your neighbor, ride lions, and chase this life."
— Jeremiah 29:11

Read This First

Just to say thanks for buying and reading my book,
I would like to connect with you!

Scan the QR Code Here:

RIDING LIONS

A Journey Through Wind, Wilderness, and the Untamed Soul

L. SETH BURCHILL

Foreword
By Jeff Bennington

My Friend, My Brother:

I'm told a Foreword to a book provides a bit of background on the Author, provides some context that could potentially give you a reason to continue reading, and then adds a bit of background that might help you get a better understanding of the person.

In a book like Seth's, I think that's important. When you read Seth's book, you're going to be hearing from him, feeling his thoughts, riding on a Harley down a desert road, and feeling the emotions he has when doing them all. That's incredible insight into a person, but it's one-sided.

It's Seth, just telling you what Seth feels and thinks.

Now, I'm not telling you that's not worth your money, but I think you need to get a picture of Seth from someone who isn't Seth. Someone who has spent countless hours listening to him, arguing with him, telling him he was stupid, telling him he was right. I've pushed Seth to be better. He's pushed me to do the same. He's also not hesitated to tell me to move on, leave it alone, it's done... and I can respect that.

Let me provide a bit more about Seth before you get into his journey through his eyes. I think it will provide the background required to understand why his thoughts might just be relevant and important for you to hear.

My journey with Seth started in the fall of 1989. I was sitting in an empty dorm room, waiting to see who this college decided would be good for me to spend my first college year with. This kid walks in, introduces himself, "Hey, I'm Seth," and as I remember it, I paused (mentally).

Something about this dude, the way he walked in, the way he wasn't worried about the moment. It was as though he just knew that whatever was going to happen from that moment was going to happen, and he wasn't really worried about it.

Now I can tell you, I liked that, and I still do today. You see, I was, and still am, a bit that way myself. We clicked immediately, like five minutes immediately. He's been my brother since that day, my best friend. He's annoyed me beyond description, provided countless moments of joy, and shared with me many highs and lows in my life and his. Brothers are that way, my sons are that way with each other. Sometimes it seems as though they've just had enough of each other, and they have, but only for a moment. Brothers have each other's backs. They're there in the good and the bad, and there's been plenty of both in this relationship. When Seth asked me to write this foreword, it was a great honor. But to be honest, I already had all the words in my head. The content was there; it was just the act of putting it on paper that was the hard part.

Ever meet someone in a public place, like a bar, a sporting event, or a company outing (pick one)? You start talking, and before long, you're hearing stories you absolutely don't believe. There's no chance this person has done that, no way he or she said that, not a chance they lived that way. I've been there, met those people, often in my line of work. I can tell when it's "getting deep" quickly. I'm paid to get a read on people quickly and determine how to work with them based on that judgment.

If Seth is that person you meet someday in a public place, at a game, a bar in St. Thomas, or wherever, just know the story he's telling is TRUE!

Now, I'm not about to tell you all those stories. That's for Seth to do. But I can tell you it's very rare to meet someone who has had the number of experiences Seth has had by the young age of fifty-five. I'll give you a teaser again, just so you'll decide you want to know more about this dude and read the rest of the book.

It's October 2001, a beautiful fall day. Nebraska vs. Oklahoma, Lincoln, Nebraska. Biggest game of the year. *College GameDay* is on site, and the city is electric. I have my ticket, and my cousin has his. Seth has no ticket. Now again, I love my brother, but when it's an hour before kickoff, I'm going into the stadium, and he's on his own. He says, "Don't worry, I'll see you inside."

Now, I'm not going to tell you the rest, because I'm hoping you'll reach out to him through whatever Riding Lions social channel you prefer and ask him to fill in the details. But just know that before that game ever started, Seth had me on the phone with Jack Arute and Barry Switzer. He stretched with the team, ON THE FIELD, and that's where I'm going to leave it.

So when you read this book, and you start to wonder, is that true, is he making this up, know IT'S TRUE! While the story is an excellent one, the better part is how hearing it, when I've told it hundreds of times, has given people a short moment of comic relief. It's impossible not to feel the moment (if the story is told right), impossible not to feel the October air, and impossible not to recognize the magnitude. It was only one month after 9/11, and security had never been tighter at events. I'm confident that when you read Seth's thoughts, feel his passion, and understand where he's coming from, you'll be better for it. You certainly aren't going to agree with it all. Heck, I don't. But it will give you a moment to reflect, think, and probably feel.

Our society, and I include myself in this, tends to judge a person quickly: by appearance, by a brief verbal exchange, and in short order, we decide whether we're in or we're not. I mentioned earlier that I do that daily in my job; it's a requirement, in my opinion, just from a time management standpoint. When a person sees Seth, cowboy hat on, jeans, Harley shirt, sunglasses, the bracelets, all of it, they may be quick to think, this guy seems a bit hard, like *what's his deal?* This guy seems a bit aggressive, maybe a bit too much. All logical and totally understandable thoughts and feelings. Seth is a bit hard, a bit too much at times, and he's certainly going to be aggressive on occasion. Both in thoughts and in speech.

Once we have those feelings, our investment in that person is almost always limited. We're done, there's no time for that. The thing Seth has taught me is that that's often a big mistake. What if a guy like Seth has something to say, feelings to share, or experiences to highlight that give you a moment to pause and reflect on your life, on the experiences you've had, and the ones you now want to have after reading his and feeling his feelings?

Now, I had it easy. I was forced to live with him those first ten months back in 1989 and for two more years until I got married. I would like to say it changed me. You see, I said we clicked immediately, but it wasn't long before I realized we're really different too. That time was impactful, important to my growth as an individual, and it still is today. I was forced to listen to Seth, feel Seth's feelings, understand his thoughts, and I'm a better man for it.

I encourage you to go into this book with no expectations. I think it's best to leave your beliefs, prejudices, and anything that might limit your ability to feel something different, on the nightstand for the evening. Take a moment to transport your mind to a highway, riding a Harley at 90 miles per hour down a desert road... I bet it feels good! Feel what it's like to be in love with your earthly father! Sound weird? It's not! Understand what it's like to be conflicted by beliefs, frightened by what might be, and comforted in what wasn't.

I love you, Brother!

Introduction

My great-grandfather was rumored to have ridden with Jesse James. In another time, I may have saddled up as well, I don't know. I know I feel his spirit. My grandmother once said I reminded her of her father.

Guess you could say I am a student of human nature and a collector of experiences. My writings are born from the seat of a Harley-Davidson, the saddle on a horse, walking the prairies and hunting the badlands of my North Dakota home, the tundras, and oceans of Alaska, crossing forty-eight states, thirty-eight on my Harley, five continents, and fifteen countries.

Guess, like the rest of us, I am a nobody, a traveller, trying to find myself in this crazy world and life.

One turn at a time.

I write when inspired by something or someone encountered. Could be a thought or an idea, could be a person or a place. Could be a shadow on the highway.

Join me as we make a trail without a compass, and no destination but thought, saddling lions.

"Buy the ticket, take the ride."
– Hunter S. Thompson

Contents

Foreword	11
Introduction	17
Why I Ride	23
I Bet God is a Cowboy	28
She Waves at Horses	31
I Got a Horse	33
Harleys in Heaven	35
Where the Coyotes Cry	37
Motorcycles	40
Have You Ever	42
Cowboy's Brush	47
My Uncle Bob	51
The Sunset Maker	56
When You Ride in the Rain	58
Small Circle	61
I Have	64
I Look West	70
Someone	73
Mississippi	75
That	78
Lost	81
My Dad	84
Burn the Ships	87
Parents	90
Cowboy Hat	93
Small Town	95

The Steady Current of Life	98
See the Effects	100
Pray for Rain	103
Life in the Mind	106
The Soul of Summer	108
Me and Mountains	111
You Know	113
Home	115
Hidden From View	117
We Are Followed	119
Your Cowboy	122
What Surrounds Us	126
Today I Watched Surfers	130
Change on the Rocks	132
To Be Significant	136
The Birds of Brooklyn	139
3002	142
About the Author	147

Why I Ride

I ride a Harley-Davidson, have since I was twenty-three years old. The question often comes up, "Why do you ride?"

Here is the answer I have come up with while riding in the wind, crossing states, lakes, running over bridges to the ocean, rolling over the snow-capped Rocky Mountains, passing hay bale-covered fields of home, and wandering through the lands of North Dakota, which the Indians called bad.

I ride to remember ... I ride to forget.

I ride to give forgiveness ... and I ride to ask for the same.

I ride to find peace ... as I ride through a loud life.

I ride to listen to the wind ... and I ride to deafen the world.

I ride to destinations ... and I ride to get lost.

I ride to think about mistakes ... and I ride knowing life is about choice.

I ride to talk to God ... and I ride to quiet the god of this world.

I ride to dry my eyes ... and I ride to smile.

I ride to think ... and I ride to numb thoughts.

I ride to break down truths ... and I ride to just accept them.

I ride to ask questions ... and I ride looking for no answers.

I ride to experience life ... and I ride to experience the subtle smells and different temperatures in a valley.

I ride to be seen ... and I ride to hide.

I ride to forget about life ... and I ride to remember how blessed I truly am in this life.

I ride and I think about making a difference ... and I ride and think about the status quo.

I ride to question those whom I have called friends ... and I ride to gain perspective on what that term truly means, and who they truly are.

I ride knowing not many would be qualified to converse or debate ... and I ride not caring either way.

I ride thinking about those who would call it a "competition" for the competitive, and tell her the same ... and I ride believing love is no game, never was to me, nor ever will be.

I ride always thinking about a boy ... and I ride knowing he will make a difference as a man.

I ride to get to family ... and I ride alone to get to no one.

I ride to places I have been with another ... and I ride to learn it is not the same when arriving.

I ride to fight those who rise up against me ... and I ride to pray for the same.

I ride knowing that life is short ... and I ride believing it will never end.

I ride to get away from those who have hurt me ... and I ride to run to those who have as well.

I ride knowing the power of the wind ... and I ride to challenge it, knowing it is strong.

I ride because few ever live ... and I ride feeling sometimes like I have died inside.

I ride to challenge the miles ... and I ride to concede the competition.

I ride to think about love ... and I ride knowing she is a cruel mirage of a mistress.

I ride wishing I didn't know now what I didn't know then ... and I ride knowing I knew all along.

I ride to embrace this life ... and I ride to let it go.

I ride to hear the sound of the motor ... and I ride to just hear the sound of silent thought.

I ride because one of the greatest men I ever knew rode with me one day ... and I ride with him still even as he has passed.

I ride to think about the city ... and I ride, missing the country.

I ride to think about emotional, real lost investments ... and I ride just considering it a sunk cost.

I ride, wondering why not me ... and I ride knowing I am hard to find, and she feels that too.

I ride having documented facts ... and I ride knowing that doesn't change anything in a heart.

I ride to get away ... and I ride to stay.

I ride to run ... and I ride to sit and wait.

I ride to listen to that still, small voice ... and I ride to yell at the top of my lungs.

I ride because I am not paying a psychologist ... and I ride knowing I have paid already.

I ride to recite scripture ... and I ride to curse true faith and time.

I ride to see God ... and I ride not looking to be seen at all.

I ride knowing that this life is a canvas on which to paint with experiences and memories ... and I ride knowing I hold the brush.

The main thing is ... I ride ... when few in life ever saddle up.

Fargo, ND - Home | Ride 2010

I Bet God is a Cowboy

Bet he is.

He opens doors and stands up when she leaves and returns to the table.

Strong and steady, a foundation in storms, a rock to hold on to. Quiet, strong, and confident in spirit.

Rides fast and free, but intentionally.

Takes care of stock and hearts alike.

Holds doors, loves open and unconditionally. Cares too much and forgives too easily.

I can see Him in an American hat, rancher's form. Skin leathered and worn from all he carries for others.

Slow to anger, quick to assist. Firm but fair. Jealous but steady. Not afraid to throw tables when merited.

Loves the mountains, waters, and plains He created equally, and what they do for the soul.

Lives with no fear for the upcoming and the past with purpose and grit.

Protects the flocks and herds from that which would upset their souls' peace and place in this world.

Allows those to wander if it be their choice and welcomes them back the same.

Knows there is a higher purpose than the day-to-day when he rises with the sun and sets the stars out at night to dot the sky.

Stands up when called upon. Sits and watches quietly, thoughtfully in a crowd.

Praises the creator daily for the created. Powerfully enjoys everything human that was gifted.

Stands in awe of the sun, moon, and the clouds above. Takes pleasure in his differing canvas of sunsets and sunrises from a painted horse on a mountain top overlooking lush green pastures.

Looks out and sees mostly good and assists with the bad.

Kills the snakes that threaten life and peace in a corral. Sees the upcoming storms over the landscape and provides shelter.

Saddles lions in Africa, and horses in the Badlands. Rides through the world, ever watchful and expectant.

Has a stable of horses and chariots of fire in the barn at the ready.

Crosses heaven on the back of a sixteen-hand steed meant for him with a golden saddle and the finest tack.

Bet he is the gateman when that day comes when we reunite with family, friends, and pets.

I bet God *is* a cowboy.

Lusk, WY | Ride 2025

She Waves at Horses

Riding down a country road, she waves and believes they see her hand.

My little backseat rider talks to them. Thinking she is heard.

Flying down the express lane on Hwy 94, a mile off over a hill, they stand, and she waves and believes they respond.

She waves because this animal touched her first in the land of the Sioux.

She waves because she is a child, and that's what children do.

She waves because innocence is still allowed, no matter what this world tries to tell us or them.

She waves because her heart is pure, and her love for that and those she loves is real and authentic, not tainted by life ... yet.

She waves because she wants to be seen—she wants connection.

She waves because God waves to us, saying I am here, and I know you see my hand.

Argyle, TX | Ride with my daughter 2023

I Got a Horse

Horses sense the heart from just feet away.

Google it; it's a fact. They sense the approaching. Your mood and demeanor speak to them about you.

Wish I did, wish I had that sense. I don't, haven't, never will. Bet you wish you did too.

It's been proven, I've proved it, choices have showed me. Probably showed you.

On me, I'm not a horse, wish I had that God-given sense.

But we saddle up and ride, that's what we do in life.

We get thrown, have a smooth trail, days on, days off.

But horses know the heart of every minute you are a part of them.

On them, around them, in their space. Think about that. Some say they do; they don't. They can't.

I like fast horses. I want to get away. Fast, disappear over a butte, a hill. Run from those I didn't sense from afar or close.

Don't want to be found, when what is found doesn't meet a horse's sense. Why share what doesn't matter to another?

Don't want to give that to anyone who didn't or doesn't deserve it.

That's why I love horses. Nice to know a being does.

They know, we don't. That makes all the difference in a life.

As we are, we can't sense a heart from two inches away, let alone yards.

Costs us, tattoos us, breaks us. Molds us, ferments us, can calcify a soul.

Saddle up, ride, and groom; a horse, it turns out, can teach you a lot.

Saw it my whole life, just learned now what it meant to be around them.

There really is something about a horse

Los Angeles, CA | 2025

Harleys in Heaven

I hope there are Harleys in heaven.

I want long roads and mountains, monuments to pass in the open air... I want my Harley in heaven.

I need to believe that I can ride fast with the wind and pass the smells and sounds of the open road ... I want my Harley in heaven.

I want to ride the skies at full throttle and look down on an imperfect world, knowing I am in the perfect place ... I want my Harley in heaven.

I was once told that heaven is a place where we are young again, and all the things we enjoyed on earth are in that place ... if that's true ... I want my Harley in heaven.

I want to see back roads, long stretches of blacktop painted into a sunset ... I want my Harley in heaven.

I think that God, who gives all and is all, would see the beauty of the thundering pipes connected to a large motor and my soul ... I want my Harley in heaven.

I yearn to ride the Badlands again in that place, and the mountains that reach to the sky ... I want my Harley in heaven.

I want to meet up with my friends and take right and left turns through the clouds together ... to nowhere, yet somehow everywhere ... I want my Harley in heaven.

I need to smell the ocean breeze as I come over a bridge and stop at a place I haven't been ... I want my Harley in heaven.

I want my rider on the back when time calls ... long hair blowing in the breeze, crossing endless landscapes of big sky home together ... I want my Harley in heaven.

I need to feel that on two wheels and with a throttle, I can meet God ... I want my Harley in heaven.

Sturgis, SD | Rally 2023

Where the Coyotes Cry

The terrain is rugged, as are the people who inhabit it.

It's not for the meek or the frail; it's reserved for the bad.

Rattlesnakes lay their skins at the altar of the sacred tipi rings of the Sioux.

How do I know this? I've seen it in the two rings on the top of our pasture.

Both situated to see miles into draws and buttes on the forever horizon.

You can't explain it, I can't either. It's just the raw truth of this land.

Generations of bones are buried here, never to be found, just to become another piece of this land.

The valleys are deep and wide, here ... where the coyotes cry.

The Indians claimed it and named it the land of many fires.

Buffalo covered it, elk, deer, too. The peaks reflect the sun's rays in the evening, and the moon's light at dark.

Here, the land doesn't sleep. It's alive. It remains awake. It watches.

The valleys are deep and wide, here ... where the coyotes cry.

The earth is red, like the devil's beard. The gravel isn't gravel at all; it's jagged like the cliffs.

Cows roam open, horses too. This place sustains them, and in doing so has sustained centuries of families too.

Hard, strong, with resolve and want to. That's what you need in these lands of bad. You need a certain armor, a fit for few.

The valleys are deep and wide here ... where the coyotes cry.

Arrowheads are in the grass, seashells off certain hills after the rain, snakes in the rocks, and lions in the dens.

It's one step to death or thousands to life. It's a risk and a reward, it's mystery and majesty.

Magic to some, as ghosts ride over the plains. Cavalries of yesterday, and the tribes they chased from draws to peak.

The valleys are deep and wide here ... where the coyotes cry.

If you look closely, you can see smoke signals rise to the sky on a distant butte to God himself.

Rivers run through this land to feed the grazing and the wild.

Canyons run dimensionally and are fragmented, jagged.

The valleys are deep and wide here ... where the coyotes cry.

This land truly is *Where the Wild Things Are*.

Their choruses echo through the hills, they pass over the sacred circles.

This is where they are, where they always have and will be.

The valleys are deep and wide here ... where the coyotes cry.

The green grass turns brown, then gray, then all covered in a blanket of white for a time.

Its winter slumber needed to nourish another year, to bring along another generation.

The awakening in the spring makes the most of the white and cold, worth the wait.

The valleys are deep and wide here ... where the coyotes cry.

This place reflects us, it's a mirror to our lives ... where the coyotes cry.

Medora, ND - Home | 2024

Motorcycles

Yeah, motorcycles are dangerous, and most choose not to ride for that reason and comment negatively on those who do.

Here is a piece of advice when talking to someone who rides. Don't talk about family members, accidents, deaths, and why you don't ride. It's not that we don't care, it's that we know the risk and reward of the wind.

We will ride anyway.

We live it.

We wave left-handed.

We find comfort in the temperature change of passing clouds as they block the sun.

The shade that an overpass provides as well as shelter from the elements.

It's not to be understood by the masses; it is reserved for the few. That's the beauty. We know not everyone gets it or ever will; we're ok with that.

As for me, LIFE is dangerous, and for that reason, I ride. I like that element, I need it, that's a challenge that builds.

I embrace the risk, and in doing so, I gain perspectives only a few will ever know through the sun, wind, and rain.

Sheridan, WY | 2022

Have You Ever

Have you ever dodged a butterfly or a bee in flight, 'cause like you, they are being carried by the wind?

Have you ever conducted a symphony of wheat across a North Dakota prairie as it answered your direction, it seemed?

Have you ever smelled the fresh water of Minnesota lake country without seeing the water, as it will appear around the next turn?

Have you ever yelled at the top of your lungs in the middle of nowhere, although nobody is listening, and you can barely hear yourself?

Have you ever passed a cotton field and swore you saw the ghosts of generations of slaves picking the cotton shell from the plant on a Louisiana backroad?

Have you ever cut through the mountains of West Virginia and got caught in a storm that shut a town down, but you had potato chips and beer for dinner with your newly found friends you met at a rest stop?

Have you ever gone into a tunnel that goes under the ocean and comes out the other side, and all you see is that blue water?

Have you ever been across the deep south and seen a rebel flag fly high behind the pine trees, and felt the current that built that symbol still flowing beneath you?

Have you ever traveled up and down the oceanfront for seven days, going nowhere yet everywhere at the same time?

Have you ever been to a beer can chicken roast in the middle of nowhere Indiana and tasted chicken like it was the first time?

Have you ever smelled a field of fresh-cut hay, shortly after it had been swathed?

Have you ever stopped alongside a road 'cause the photo opportunity in front of you feels like your life?

Have you ever shaken hands with someone at 80 mph in the open air 'cause you share the same spirit?

Have you ever shared something with a stranger because you could make a memory for them?

Have you ever seen a Nebraska skyline and river valley that, if you look close enough, you can see the cavalry riding through?

Have you ever been to the land of the Seminole, and your senses smelled the pipe smoke of the elders as you crossed their land?

Have you ever stopped at an oyster bar on the Florida Gulf Coast and partook of the same oysters that feed the nation, except you get them right off the boat?

Have you ever waved at people with your left hand dropped down to your side, and felt a brotherhood though you have never met them and will never see them again …

Have you ever crossed bridges that extend for miles over open water?

Have you ever stopped to take a picture of a town 'cause the road sign said *"Faith,"* and you were looking for a sign?

Have you ever taken a wrong road for a hundred miles, and turns out it was a better option after all?

Have you ever crossed through Cajun country and seen alligators in a skiff freshly caught from the bayou?

Have you ever looked out over the badlands into a canyon and felt you saw over the heat lines the silhouettes of a Sioux hunting party riding bareback, horses colored for the hunt alongside a painted butte?

Have you ever cried when you saw your state sign as you entered it with a light rain glassing over the prairies?

Have you ever hung your jeans up on a doorknob to wear the next day, although they are soiled, 'cause your grandpa did the same thing, his soiled from the farm, yours from the road?

Have you ever felt like you wished a day could last a lifetime, based on what you experienced with every sense you were given?

Have you ever looked into the sky and talked to those who left you too early, and you hope they see you flying down the road you find yourself on now , and are looking down with pride?

I have, and much more, on the two wheels of my Harley, and the states most fly over, I ride through, and experience the individual beauty and uniqueness up close and personal. The filters of books and media don't compare.

So, excuse my questioning nature when I'm asked, "Why ride?" I ride to experience the above and more, riding through this world to see it, touch it, smell it ... it is the only way I know to live.

A man is dead in his spirit without the desire for learning and adventure through new experiences. I am not dead yet, and I choose to experience. That's why I will ride.

Scottsbluff, NE | Ride 2022

Cowboy's Brush

I'd rather be a cowboy than anything.

We will ride through the woke, or anything really. When you think about it, all that is, or isn't, in the field.

Just truth, nothing more, nothing less. You want it, you can ask, that is what you will get.

So many people in this life want to make it out to *what* they are instead of *who* they are.

Cowboys don't.

We are who we are, you take it or you don't. Either is respected, but nothing is changed.

We will be who we are, and you will be who you are, and in the end, I guess we will see.

But I have never seen the cowboy code not make heaven.

In the end, all we take are people with us to that place.

Love God.

Love your neighbor.

Love the animals we have been entrusted to keep, and to live off.

Love each other, and ride free in this short life.

Name a rodeo that doesn't have a prayer … Been to them all, can't name one.

I think God shines on that, shines on those cowboys and cowgirls, the animals, cause I guess they know.

Look at any interview in the NFR in the heart of Sin City, count the times God isn't mentioned. It may be on one finger, more than likely none.

It's because country matters, horses and stock, and the parents that raise them with the reins, through the rains, and the droughts alike.

God, manners, code, country—it is what we were built on.

The hats matter, they aren't for show, they are for class, honor, and respect. In short for God.

You go to a steak house in Fort Worth, it's the only hat you can wear at the table. *Ask me how I know.*

Can't do that in Dallas, although Pappas allowed me, Bobs always does. He's a dude. A horse guy.

Yeah, the code matters.

That's why we ride and choose who to ride with.

Some are hands, some fall off. We still hang in the saddle.

Life is the ride, the proper cinch, saddle, bit and reins, and tribe.

Should teach you to love God.

Love your neighbor.

Don't cheat.

Be true.

Matter to your wife or husband and children. Be selfless, not selfish.

Show up.

Be real.

Be authentic.

Live your life out loud and on purpose.

Have a track record.

In short, matter, or don't.

Let the brushes of your life tell you.

Allow the canvas to show.

Your choice of what the brush strokes look like. You hold and guide them.

The lines won't be perfect; we weren't created to be.

But, they will tell you who you are, not what you seemed to be, or who people thought you were.

Mirrors will do the same.

They watched the entire ride.

The strokes of your life leave a vivid image.

When you get turned out to eternity's pasture.

Make sure you held.

A cowboy's brush.

Taos, NM | Ride West 2025

My Uncle Bob

Ninety percent of life and relationships is showing up.

I didn't ask and haven't talked much about the funeral since I got back to my family, but I would be willing to bet people showed up for my Uncle Bob on the day his life was honored.

They showed up 'cause he showed up for everyone in that area and beyond. He showed up for no other reason than that, to him, that was what you do for people, that is how you live, that is what matters.

I know he showed up in my life. His selfless attitude and giving, humble nature were to be admired, and I will cherish the memories that he gave me.

I heard there was no open mic at the funeral. That pisses me off. (Further, I heard that it was his wish not to have one, OF COURSE!

That was his humbleness and nature! He deserved that hot mic and people sharing memories.)

If I had been there, I can promise you the mic would have been in my hand. I would have spoken about a man I loved who loved me. With Grandma, Grandpa, our country family tree, and the rest of the family past hanging on a cloud and listening, I would have told whoever was there and upstairs what I loved about my Uncle Bob, what I love about being the blood of my father, and how he embodied everything that matters in life that makes our name great. How real and authentic, humble people like him are rare and to be treasured.

He had a way about him that made you feel more important than you were when you talked to him. His smile, sideways grin, voice, laugh, honest nature, strong handshake, forearms bigger than my arms, not an enemy in the world demeanor mattered.

He always asked me about my life when I saw him … always. When he talked, smiled, and encouraged me in his nonverbal way. It built me and formed foundations.

I don't know a person who matters in life who could say a bad thing about the man. The uncle I knew was honest to a fault, hardworking, a man's man, who was there for his family and friends in Valley City and beyond.

I have so many fond memories of Uncle Bob. I loved hanging out with him and the rest of my dad's brothers growing up. It made me feel good, it gave me confidence, and it taught me a sense of family and what that feels like. Brothers are special, and they share a special bond … I loved being a part of it; they all touched my soul.

The farm off the peak interchange on I-94 molded me. No matter where I go, whenever anyone asks me where I am from, I tell them I am from North Dakota. Love the state, the people, and our family; that's where you find the Uncle Bobs in life.

It's where I grew up. It's where I heard Uncle Bob drop the f-bomb when we were hauling cattle to my Uncles and the trailer started sliding down the hill on their road 'cause we had just had a blizzard and it was wintertime, and the gravel was glare ice. Oh, and Dad was behind us.

In life, I don't trust anyone unless I hear them cuss once in a while, so Dad, you know I trust you. Hell, up until that moment, I thought he was perfect. It's where I could hear Dad and Uncle Bob working on equipment, yelling at me and each other for God knows what, and teaching me to drive a combine, truck, and tractor, and then ride horses at my other uncle's (I miss Sassy Boy).

It's where I drove a grain truck to Section 9 and saw a combine way off course going across swaths ... and sped the Chevrolet truck up fast enough to get ahead of the combine to jump on ... and found my Uncle Bob sleeping at the wheel. YES, that is true! Ask Dad. I told him as soon as I got back to the yard that day.

In the cab of that same combine was where I heard my uncle say to me when I told him I was hungry, "When I get hungry, I take a drink of water." Then he handed me the thermos. I NEVER forgot that, or the Allis-Chalmers combines I learned to drive when I didn't even have a license.

Just like I will never forget buying him probably the only two beers he had in his life (Coors Light) on a 100-plus degree day when Dad, I, and Uncle Bob cleaned out Grandpa's garage. That was a Fourth of July break, and I remember my friends and girlfriend going to the lake and wanting me to go. I am SO glad I didn't because my dad, Uncle Bob, and I had a great day together. Funny, the days in life that one remembers sometimes. Even before his passing, that day stuck in my mind as one of the top five in my life.

I could write forever, but I will close with this. This past summer, when we all met at the cabin, was special. It meant something. Our family of North Dakotans means something to the world we encounter and live in, and we should matter to each other. Memories and family are all we have in life, with the exception of God, who gives both and all.

When I was returning home on my Harley, I ran into Uncle Bob at a gas station in Bismarck. Even though I am grown, Uncle Bob told me to be sure to be careful and come back home more often.

I hugged him and told him I loved him and would be fine. I never thought that would be the last time I saw him.

Side note on that: I loved to watch my uncle with my sisters, my niece and nephew, and my mom. He hugged them harder, and I loved that he was a man's man and that was his way, and, in some ways, our family way. One thing is for sure: he loved kids, and kids loved him.

I hate cancer; it makes me want to use a stronger word, and I hate that it took a good man way too soon, that I will miss. I hate that now that he's gone, he doesn't know how I truly felt about him and the impact he had on my life. I hate that I never got to tell him in person. No matter what philosophers, Christians, atheists, the scholars of this life, or anyone says, cancer has no explanation, has no point, has no purpose, and I have a question for God when I join my uncle.

So, Uncle Bob, tell Grandma I am sorry for some of the language (I can hear her saying, "Seth, you be nice") and laugh with Grandpa for me about it. I love you and am thankful that you were a significant part of this man's life; I will see you in time.

Save me a swig of water from that thermos, and I will bring the beer.

Santiago, Chile | 2012

The Sunset Maker

You paint the skies with a movement of your finger ... You are the sunset maker.

Each one in the history of the canvas ... different ... You are the sunset maker.

Captivating Your people for generations, the settlers and the upper class of today alike ... You are the sunset maker.

Cotton candy or fire red and yellow or another from Your palette. You alone choose the colors of the dusk ... You are the sunset maker.

An end to the day is evidence of Your power and craftsmanship to an audience of us...You are the sunset maker.

You provide the gift of the end of a day and the promise of another beautiful blink of an eye nightly ... You are the sunset maker.

Opacarophiles stand in awe when the sun of the day lowers, framed pictures in mind...You are the sunset maker.

We are undeserving takers of a free gallery showing every evening at dusk from Your endless creative touch ... You are the sunset maker.

Thank You for never making us pay for this or our life as we should ... You are the sunset maker.

Phoenix, AZ | 2024

When You Ride in the Rain

When you ride in the rain, you are forced to understand life.

In the middle of a trip, states away from home, and the weather in the ride dictates the conditions, you have one choice ... to ride on.

Rain, sleet, snow, hail. You ride through it.

You get that you aren't in control; the skies aren't yours to own, you just rent.

Yours is to persevere, to ride through the storm. Like life, you have to face it and adapt.

Every groove and dry spot on the road is now yours to find through foggy glasses and passing traffic. Rain filling your glasses, semis blinding you as they pass.

As in life, you have to ride it out.

You stop more to reset, recharge. Then ride.

It's not easy, it's not intended to be. Your lenses drip with the rain, like your life's lens does in storms of life.

The view isn't clear, your hands are numb, and the windshield is now both for the wind and to give your hands a break from the elements.

But, you ride on.

You ride on because clouds change, the rain will stop, storms will pass. The sun will shine; you will just have to find it another day, chase it, believe it will come out again.

There are mountain passes ahead to be seen, monuments to view, canyons to cross.

When the sun finally shows, you truly understand thankfulness, the blessings of the road, the path, in short, God.

You will see it in the mountains the next day, across the land of red with monuments and buttes, when you chase it, you will find it and be found.

Every raindrop, sleet BB, and snowflake will be worth the *now* view.

Because storms pass, it is in their nature. It's the constant.

So is the sun—it rises, shines, sets, it's in its nature.

So the above is in the nature and is woven into the fabric of our lives.

We were built for storms; we are prepared for the rain and the storms. He told us they would come.

He also told us the Son would rise, and the storms would pass by once again as well.

That's the promise; that's the light we chase, and that chases us, much like the sun.

The constant in our storms is Him.

That is why we need to chase the light. The light owns the darkness over the storms, the light will pierce the clouds.

When you have ridden in the rain, you appreciate the light more.

You see the beauty, you chase it now and will again.

The light is why you ride.

The storms are what you ride through to find it.

Rogers, AR | Bikers, Blues, BBQ Rally 2023

Small Circle

My circle is small.

There is family, and those I chose as family, really all that matters.

The only things you have in life are memories and experiences from this trip that is the blink of an eye. The only thing you take to heaven are people you make memories and share experiences with.

That eye blink gives you perspective, gives you strength in the chaos of the storm, gives you hope that the palace you're destined for is under construction.

When someone takes a punch in this life and in my circle, it hits different.

It causes you to pause and think about living in this place without them; it hurts. It should.

Nobody likes bad news; that is a fact. No matter what type of human you are.

When it comes to your family and friends, that news gets a lot of press in your mind.

It does mine, at least.

I pray harder, think deeper, wander back further, pull out old memories and experiences from the file.

I come to a realization and consider how small and insignificant I am in a world that will never request my permission to make changes or deviate from the serene glass waters. I realize how not in control I am. It is then I am thankful for the Captain.

I realize my place more, what is important, what isn't, who is, who isn't.

Reflection changes you a little, it's meant to.

Forces you to let go, control what you can control, allow the rest to be the rest, "Let go and let God." I've heard that my whole life.

But your grip is tighter when it comes to your circle; you ride the full eight seconds ... you bleed from the rope.

It's hard to think about future memories and experiences made with a line out of the circle.

Hard to consider life without the whole sphere intact.

So I will pray harder, I will love stronger, I will be intentional with the few.

I will live with those I have chosen to love and call my family here.

I will be purposeful and intentional with my relationships.

Daily.

I will live for the next memory and experiences ... in my small circle.

Eldora, OH | World 100 Late Model Dirt Track Race Camp 2022

I Have

Have you ever seen your silhouette at 90 miles an hour on the side of a Kansas cornfield?

I have ...

Have you ever heard the echo of motorcycle pipes through a South Dakota canyon like the sounds of the buffalo stampeding lifetimes before?

I have ...

Have you ever stopped at the side of the road because you swore you could see Indians crossing a Nebraska river valley with open plains ahead?

I have ...

Have you ever seen a painted land at full throttle so bad the namesake carries the same name to describe what you are witnessing?

I have ...

Have you ever taken shelter from a Midwest storm under a tree with no cover in sight or help coming, just prayers offered?

I have ...

Have you ever stopped at a no-place restaurant in the middle of nowhere and tasted the fresh catch of the day on a Florida coastline you would swear God was still writing in the sand?

I have ...

Have you ever come around a corner to a herd of bison, and your sound placed you in a stare down with the herd's leader?

I have ...

Have you ever been chased by the same storm for three states, with each gas stop a NASCAR-like pit stop to stay ahead?

I have ...

Have you ever slept on a couch in a hotel chain you have been to thousands of times because they were sold out, and the storm caught up?

I have ...

Have you ever crossed the mountains of Colorado and found yourself on a mining road only meant for miners that was not supposed to be on a map—forty miles ... four miles per hour?

I have ...

Have you ever stopped at a rest area alone, then were asked to join a group, then traveled five states with your new friends?

I have ...

Have you ever had hail hit you in the face like BBs and marbles on a highway cutting through the mountains when the weather did not want you to pass?

I have ...

Have you ever taken shelter from a storm ... two hotel rooms ... thirty strangers ... no food in town except for gas station chips and beer ... to multiply like the loaves and the fish for your brothers and sisters of the road?

I have ...

Have you ever felt the sun's rays so hot on your flesh that you believed that you had gained an armor coating and lost your flesh?

I have ...

Have you ever walked into a dealership with your family and seen them transformed by the myth they were always told but had to experience to believe?

I have ...

Have you ever been rained on so hard your glasses pool, accepting the rain that blurs your vision, lifting to empty a mile at a time?

I have ...

Have you ever purchased your first Harley at twenty-three, and your first thought was to take it to the man who taught you to ride, who taught you everything, and watched as he disappeared wide open down the block for an hour?

I have ...

Have you ever tucked in behind a semi for warmth and protection from deer passing in the night and felt that you were back in the womb, safe from the surrounding world?

I have ...

Have you ever just taken off with no destination but thought and right and left turns and found yourself where you were meant to be for that day?

I have ...

Have you ever viewed the road as your psychologist and spoken to the wind as it rushes past your head, taking the thoughts withheld and the worries with it past you, behind you, gone?

I have ...

Have you ever seen the joy of a child's eye and smile as you ask them if they would like to sit on a machine they don't understand, but are somewhat drawn to, like their parents, who are allowing and are drawn to the same?

I have ...

Have you ever watched an owl leave its perch and swoop in front of you on an Arkansas White Mountain back road and realized that bird could have just taken your life with its wings?

I have ...

Have you ever ridden to a destination, numb from the world and its deeds, thinking of nothing and everything as the miles pass? I have ...

Have you ever walked into a place where the only thing you have in common is the two wheels and steel you just put the kickstand down on, and you felt a sense of family, belonging?

I have ...

Have you ever prayed throttle down, asking the God that made all that you are passing and the wind that is carrying you, and somehow found a listening ear?

I have ...

Have you ever had a stranger look at you across a table in a crowded room and tell you their struggles and their redemption just because you were clad in the same leather?

I have ...

Have you ever rushed from the top of a West Virginia mountain down into the valley and seen the parallels of the temperature drop mirror your life?

I have ...

Have you ever ridden the hill country of Texas down farm roads of the sisters and seen the maker's fingerprint on a landscape?

I have ...

Have you ever hugged people you've only ridden with ... only met on the road ... and now it's your exit, and they have miles to go, and their tears flow?

I have ...

I've done this all from the seat of my Harley ... those who know, understand. Those who don't, you're always invited to chase the wind and find yourself with us.

Apalachicola, FL | Ride 2013

I Look West

Every morning and every night, before I close my eyes, I look West.

I see the sunset West and think of sunsets and how they will forever have a new meaning 'cause she loves them.

I wonder if I ever mattered ... If I ever was loved ... If I ever was respected.

Sometimes I clear my eyes. Empty on my face, void of meaning, and full of thoughts.

Memories I can't let go of, times I can't erase. West is where they are. The price of memories is regret, a useless emotion.

West is where she is. West is where my heart won't leave. It's stuck in neutral and runs 24/7.

A transmission of the mind and of a time when life was full and mattered more, it seemed.

A family that was adopted as my own, souls that showed up out of the blue, that are now a part of me.

Now gone. Gone from our lives, as now we are strangers again. Strangers who view the same sunsets but separately.

I will never know or understand. This depth is foreign to me. It's deeper than I've ever gone. I can't see the surface as I fall; it gets darker.

Prayers flow to the West with the winds; they evaporate as they lift and are offered up. West is where the whiskey failed to drown it all.

West is where she is. West is where my heart is. West is the blessing and the curse.

West is where I look, and I wonder for how long. How long until I find rest in another direction and find hope?

I don't know. Questions never leave, I find no rest in North, South, or East. I find no rest period.

I pray I do because reactions and choices made looking West are foreign to me. I've never seen that side of me.

Tells me West mattered, it meant something. It built me for a time, and now it destroys.

So tomorrow I will awaken with the sun rising East but thoughts West, and chase the sunset the same.

A dagger to the heart, a direction forever written on my soul. The spring rains haven't washed away, haven't cleansed the spirit.

West is a girl. West is questions. West is unanswered prayers. West was " I need time," and now time is all there is.

Was West just a mirage, a betrayal from the beloved, thought, word, and deed? Or was there water?

Eyes have no eraser, no back button, no delete. Eyes find truth. Sight files away.

Was West a lie?

West will forever remain a question.

West may never have or give an answer.

Vancouver, British Columbia | 2025

Someone

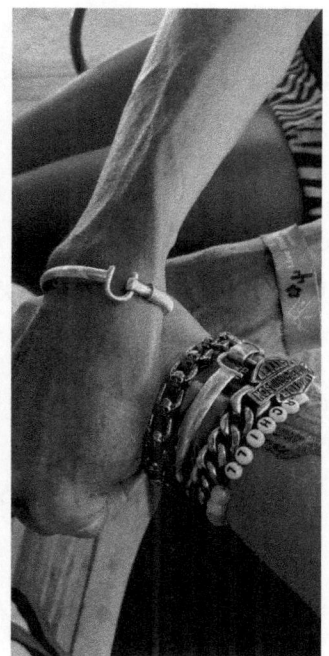

We all need someone.

Someone to tell about our wins, someone to tell about our losses ... someone.

Someone to be a witness to our live ... to be beside us, around us, in us. Inked on our soul ... someone.

Someone to give us the confidence to live and to move forward. Someone to rein us in ... someone.

Someone to talk about nothing and everything ... someone.

Someone to trust in, someone to share our secrets with, someone to ride or die with on life's highways ... someone.

Someone to laugh with. Someone to fall with time like the sands in an hourglass ... someone.

Someone to show us what love is and that it really is a real thing, and we can fall ... we're allowed ... someone.

My someone's prayer is you, wherever you are. And when that gift is received, it will never be sent back, will never be returned, it won't ever be taken for granted. It will always be guarded, nourished, and the flame won't ever go out.

Not with my someone, you.

Charlotte Amalie, St. Thomas USVI | 2023

Mississippi

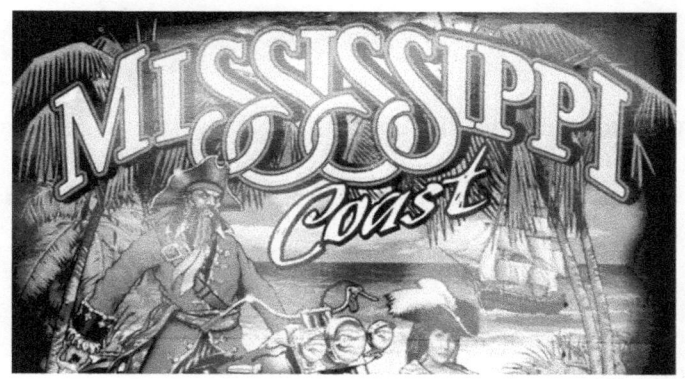

It's not just a state ...

Or a river ...

She's a girl ...

A girl whose heart flows like that river ...

Whose spirit is as strong as that state ...

But she's more.

She's more than the river whose current feeds a nation ...

She's more than the state that serves as the dividing line for the East and the West ...

She's special ...

She's real ...

She's strong …

She's unlike anything I've experienced in any state …

Or any time on a river.

She's different …

She matters to strangers she cares for and who matter to her …

She matters to the family she created, and who, like her, are strong …

She's a lighthouse in a dark place …

She's a lifeline to many …

She's special …

She's significant in an insignificant world …

She's rain, she's sun; she stands in storms daily …

She's an angel who carries with wings of care …

She's the fire that burns for the cold …

No, Mississippi isn't just a state …

Isn't just a river …

She's more significant than both …

She's a girl who matters to the masses …

Who matters to me ...

Pray she's a love, and not a lesson.

Kanab, UT | 2023

That

You want to be That.

That ... someone thinks about.

That ... someone wants in their life.

That ... someone needs.

That ... someone desires.

That ... someone can't imagine life without.

That ... someone's only.

That ... someone says goodnight to.

That ... someone can talk unedited and real.

That ... someone who knows you and loves you anyway.

That... someone who laughs at life with you.

That ... someone who cries about that same life.

That ... someone who judges nobody but holds true to truths.

That ... someone who loves family and knows what that means.

That ... someone who knows this life is a blink of an eye adventure.

That ... someone who gets it.

That ... someone's biggest fan.

That ... someone's strongest shoulder.

That ... someone's keeper of secrets.

That ... someone's compass.

That ...someone who throws pasts into the depths of the deepest ocean.

That ... someone who lives out loud and on purpose.

That ... someone who loves like Jesus does.

That ... someone who gets that life isn't fair, never will be, and there is no scorecard.

That ... someone who believes the light at the end of the tunnel isn't an oncoming train.

That ... someone who believes when there is no reason to.

That ... someone who takes life as is, no excuses, no regrets, which in itself is a useless emotion.

That ... someone who understands we all have scars, but they don't define.

That ... someone who sees the windshield, not the rearview.

That ... someone who loves unconditionally and trusts that's enough.

That ... someone who sees the world through a child's eye.

That ... someone who sees God in the seasons.

That ... someone who sees God in those same seasons of their life.

That ... someone who accepts the cruel evils and stands against them.

That ... someone who smells the rain and knows it is designed for good.

That ... someone who views the world as a tapestry, and we are the weavers.

That ... someone who is faithful, honest, and unedited.

That ... is it.

Anchorage, AK | 2022

Lost

You ever been lost when you're at home?

Wander room to room, wonder where you are or where you ever were, and if it mattered at all.

Question everything and everyone, say things out of character because it changed you ... lost does that. It changes someone.

It changes your perspective on life, on people ... because they say they care but you know they don't, maybe never did, easy for them to say, to move on ... still leaves you lost.

Learn they were a lie, their life too, wonder what was ever true, learn not much was, now for the next to find out, the saying is true, once a ... Lost.

Sometimes, lost is a good place to find yourself, on the seat of a Harley has been the best place for me to be when I'm lost, not my mind. It doesn't work like that.

The price of memories is always regret when lost—lost in feeling, thought, life, choices.

People want to be "happy," only to learn it's a temporary emotion. It feeds on questions that beg for attention, but still stays temporary, always will. That is by design, by the designer.

True joy in life comes from a source far above us, that points us in a direction where lost isn't part of the equation. Where memories aren't daggers that stab the soul.

I trust few, because most leave you lost, and keep you in that state based on their blurred view of reality and love.

Lowering expectations of people is the best way to insulate yourself, protect yourself from those who push you to lose.

The amber color in a glass and the smoke rolling off your fingers through your lungs won't find you either.

Just like the seat of a Harley and intersection options, you have to choose what road you believe will bring you back to found.

Some people never find it, some just keep taking turns. Some like lost, when they aren't found, they can't be loved, they can't be hurt, they can't matter.

The only lost I prefer is on two wheels, where any direction chosen with a turn is found to me.

I prefer to be found. Found matters in life. I think found is who we were created to be.

Found is what He wants for us in this shattered glass view of our reflection in this place that was never meant to be our home.

You have to choose to be found. Found by Him and what He wants for your life.

We aren't in a place in this blink and moment here to understand it.

Long Beach, CA | 2025

My Dad

A lifetime North Dakotan, son of a farmer in Valley City, smart, athletic, mechanically minded, loyal, honest, a man's man. That's who he is and my stock.

If you ever meet my dad or have met him and don't like him, you don't like people. The conversation is mute, and you're wrong.

I can't say that about myself. I can't.

My Dad taught me right from wrong. He didn't just tell me, he showed me. Showed me how to be a man, care for women, care for the land, care in general. That's what REAL men do.

Rare thing these days, I know I was fortunate.

My dad taught me to drive when I was eight, and cussed me for pulling the clutch. Rode me and my sisters around in the back of a pickup bed since I can remember. Disciplined on the things that mattered; let go of the boy's choices that didn't.

Bought me my first can of chewing tobacco when I was in sixth grade. We were going to a rodeo, showed me how to pinch and gum. He didn't know I would take it to school, but that's another story. He had my back.

Smoked a pipe, smoked cigars and, I guess, better cigarettes when I made the mistake of letting him open the glove box and see my paltry Camel lights when I was twenty-three in my first truck. "What is this? If you're going to smoke, smoke. I used to smoke Camel 'bares' and Pall Malls." Sorry, Dad, my filtered lights aren't good enough.

I'm not an addict, I still chew when I want to, smoke cigars the same, who cares, as I write this, you probably did too, if you didn't, congratulations, you will die anyways.

He wasn't always right, but he knew what it took to make a man. I see that now; I'm thankful I do. His resume is strong. That's been proven.

Married fifty-four years, lifetime high school basketball scoring record for North Dakota High School basketball, although he wouldn't let the news media or anyone interview him about that feat. Gearhead and hot rod builder. Arctic cat racing team member, sales manager, crack shot with a rifle, great friend to a few close.

He's accomplished.

Took me on sales calls when I was ten. I stayed in hotels, ate with him and customers, hunted, golfed, went to professional baseball, football, and hockey games. He was invested in me. Sales became my career.

Taught me to throw, catch, golf, shoot a basketball, shoot and handle a gun, hunt and catch and filet fish, drive, love God, and treat people ... that's all I needed.

More than anything, he taught me how to live, to be a man, to care, to love, and to discern. That's what he did.

There aren't enough words to write to describe him. I just wanted to give you a snapshot of a man and life, and how to live. You and I, who are reading, will be better for this.

He's my hero, he's my best friend, he's my dad.

We all need something to chase, something to strive for, something to leave, something to be.

He is the last paragraph to me.

Las Vegas, NV | 2021

Burn the Ships

We all have them.

Boats lost at sea in our minds. Sails that hang for no reason. Past relationships, wrong choices, doubts, fears, anxieties of the unknown and unfounded. We have ships that we allow to stay afloat in our head for no real reason or purpose ...

Burn the ships.

When the god of today enters the picture, those boats catch a current ... a breeze ... a false assistance that serves nothing ... a mission of destruction cast in the guise of help ...

Burn the ships.

Toxic people, toxic culture, a world that is so lost it thinks it can find itself in itself. It believes "self" is all you need ... why allow it to float ...

Burn the ships.

When we burn the ships of our lives ... the ships that once sailed ... once guided ... ones we thought were compass-driven, only to learn they were rudderless ... when we burn those ships, we find our islands ... our paradises, our sanctuaries.

Burn the ships.

When we learn that we were fearfully and wonderfully made for a life to be lived out loud and on purpose with a single Captain, we have a seaworthy ship worthy of the waters and the oncoming swells, we have a bow worthy of being christened ...

We are one of one in this entire universe, a miracle made to float, made to sail, made to capture the wind.

Burn the ships.

Monterrey, Mexico | 2020

"If you're going to be a friend,
be a friend like Skoal, always there in a pinch.
If you're gonna love a woman,
you got to love her like a Chevy, buddy, steady like a rock.
If something's on your mind,
got somethin' to say,
do it like your Browning, try to shoot 'em straight.
Hell, just look around you,
be Skoal, Chevy, and Browning."

– Morgan Wallen: Skoal, Chevy, and Browning

Parents

I often hear my friends tell me how wonderful their kids, now adults, have turned out to be as people.

My initial honest response in my mind is, *Well, look in the mirror; that's you being lived out now in your children. Why are you surprised? You are great people. I'm not surprised, why should you be?*

Well, it is always wonderful to hear the credit belongs to the parents—it belongs to you.

That's your resume of a job well done; that's your tattoo on a life that is being well lived.

Oftentimes in life and vocation and in competition, we think and see the WIN. But we forget about the work, the sacrifice, the effort that went behind it.

In games and sports, we often forget about the long hours in the weight room, the long runs to build ourselves, the hills we ran to strengthen us for battle. We forget about the very foundation and preparation that prepared us to succeed on the field, on the ice, on the court.

In work, we forget about the studies in college that led us and trained our minds for what was ahead to succeed. We don't go back to those libraries enough where we shaped our future life, and our mentality was formed and built to WIN.

We need to.

We need to slow down and take credit for what we did right, what we sacrificed in time, and sweat equity to pay for what we have.

We NEED to take credit.

'Cause the bullets that fly and the arrows in the air of life will come. Storms will come; the rain will fall. That isn't a promise, it's a fact ... and they will be prepared ... you fashioned them for the fires.

BUT we are prepared, and we have prepared ours for the same. WE are the mold, through Christ, who prepared us for victory.

Take credit. Have confidence in the fact that YOU are the coach who leads your kids to life's victories.

Good parents don't do that enough.

Nashville, TN | 2023

Cowboy Hat

I wear a cowboy hat daily in my personal life or business.

Why? Because of Dad. Best man I know or will ever know. He does, so I do. The only reason.

Not our horses or the country lifestyle our family has lived for generations ... it's him.

It has separated me, the corporate world had to accept it; didn't give them the choice.

Makes me feel like him, the farm, our horses. North Dakota.

That's why. Anyone who meets me doesn't ask, it fits. They know.

My roots run deep. They feel it, see it, they understand and feel. It's known.

I'm not him. He's better than me. Raised me to be better than him, a tall task. I will never be.

Will still wear the hat every day of my life; it connects me to the greatest man in my life. It connects me to the state and farm and the lands of bad ... it connects me to home and him.

More of a cowboy than I will ever be. But I need that fingerprint of him. I need to feel I am in the palm of my earthly father's hand.

It has always built me, challenged me, and confused me at times, but I see now.

He knew. Cowboys always do.

Cleveland, OH | 2021

Small Town

Things move slower, the people do too, the biscuits at the cafe are homemade, they're better.

When you arrive, you're a stranger; they know it. When you leave, you aren't.

Life is right in these towns. God is present. The little church on the corner is full on Sundays.

The streets are quiet day or night, the shops too, save for the locals or weary nomads passing through.

Generations meet on a corner or in a bar after five when the work is done or the commute to the city has been conquered for another day.

The high school team is the celebrity of the town, the players for the year are gods; their girlfriends wear their jackets. Their pictures and schedules dot the restaurant walls. Fridays are sacred in the fall.

The water towers are freshly painted, graffiti isn't allowed, and beer cans from the Friday night country party are thrown in the back of pickups. The local police know and are known.

The window view is livestock and lush fields of green. This is theirs too. Fences are kept and mended; buildings and barns glisten in the morning sun and the evening sunset.

You feel a sense of mystery when you visit and stop in a local cafe. People communicate, phones aren't in their hands, and aren't answered much.

Doors aren't locked, guns are ... locked and loaded. There isn't trouble; it's guarded and watched by the residents.

There is a sense of pride you feel from the inhabitants. You feel this is theirs, and you're welcomed after the first wondering stares pass.

Country music plays in the background everywhere. The John Deere implements have the freshest coffee for customers.

Grass is mowed, the streets are clean. Their care and the pride taken are noticeable.

Every corner is a picture, as if Norman Rockwell used them as a canvas to paint the way life is meant to be lived.

The bread is fresh—you can smell it—and every restaurant feels Michelin star-like. The chefs of the establishments know food, they know what their people like, and what you will learn to appreciate.

It's not a tourist trap. It is a trap of the mind and the senses you don't mind being caught in.

You put the kickstand down when you see a local children's lemonade stand. You pay them twenty dollars for a ten-cent advertised cup; you feel you owe it somehow. The smiles cover it.

People ask about your bike, children are allowed to sit, their parents are thankful for the shared experience, you are thankful for the conversation about chrome and paint.

When you leave, it's as if you were never there. But you were, and now that small town is a part of you.

The images of the way life was meant to be lived are filled; you feel full.

Turning right out of town when you throttle down, you think, *I need this, if but only for a time.* Everyone does.

Miles down the road and a few turns and the city skyline appears; the traffic isn't tractors and combines anymore, people drive on their phones.

You immediately miss it, as the sounds grow louder, the noise of the city roars over the sound of your pipes. The streets are dirty again.

Then you wonder ... why did I leave?

Pilot Point, TX | 2025

The Steady Current of Life

I am sitting riverside on a cold, crisp day. The sun is out, the traffic passes by the bridges, home for the weekend, and the water flows.

When I look out at the river, I notice something that strikes me as profound, I guess you might say. With the current, there are logs, trash, birds, and other objects that drift. Looking out, I can see them for a bit, a few moments, but then they are carried downstream out of sight.

It strikes me that that is life, that is the destination of past choices and decisions made, good or bad. They all flow away out of sight, and the new clear water comes with its own elements of choice and chance. Could have trash, could be clear, still will flow, and continue to move to a yesterday that will never be today or tomorrow.

Guess it is refreshing to know that with time and the current of life, we can be free to see a clearer view and a new chance at significance, free from the trash and debris of the past.

If we let the past define us instead of describe us, we forfeit the wonderful chance that is today and the tomorrows of the rest of our lives.

Shreveport, LA | 2010

See the Effects

I awoke this morning standing on the deck to a crisp breeze blowing in tree country. Looking at the tops of the trees and hearing the wind that moved them, something hit me.

We can only see the effects of the wind, but we can't see the wind. We can hear the power, we can see the result, but we can't physically see the wind itself.

Standing there like I have so many times before, I started to think of other things and objects I have seen the wind move in my life. Wheat fields that connect by section lines on the North Dakota countryside, dead tree branches creaking in the middle of a ten-below-zero day as I stalked deer in Montana, or white caps that become a force on a lake and crash into the shore with nothing visible pushing them, but the force is there driving them.

I am reminded, as I see the effects of the wind in the tops of these trees, that the wind is a lot like God and faith. We cannot see Him or faith, but we can see His effects and our faith if we choose to take the time to look.

I have often believed that there are no coincidences in life, that, like so many people using the trite phrase "Everything happens for a reason," Godly coincidences can be all around us and meet us at our point of need if we look for them.

Once we see them, it is then our choice to believe that the effects are real and embrace the unseen touch that is reaching down to tell us, "It is I." Look and you will see that I can become visible in your life, and you can feel the effects of my leading if you make the choice to believe.

There is an empty feeling sometimes when we struggle with daily life, and we fail to see the coincidences where an unseen God is working. It is my belief that if you are seeking answers and there are signs that flash in front of you in daily life that beam brightly with coincidental truth and direction, God has done his job.

Now the choice is yours: step out in faith, or don't, choose to believe, or don't, follow the effects of Godly coincidence and trust in the unseen adventure of faith he has for you, or don't.

When we base our decisions on ourselves, on our feelings, on our circumstances, we reject the only power that, although unseen, holds the answers.

In short, God has shown us; now it's up to us. His job is completed; do we believe and follow, or trust in ourselves like we have so many times before, only to see nothing and feel the same?

Look for the effects of the unseen, and scan your daily life for Godly coincidental answers. You may find that the unseen will reveal the lighted path and lead you on the road where you were predestined to go.

The same force that moves the tops of these trees can move you and me, if we allow. It's a yes or no, but His job has been completed; we should expect nothing more.

West Monroe, LA | 2011

Pray for Rain

It has been raining for five days straight now, the ground is saturated, and the youth football team's uniforms, cleats, socks, and helmets carry the field with them in muddy form.

There is something about rain that cleanses, renews, and washes our souls, it seems. I often have walked in the middle of a rainstorm and talked with God, or talked out loud to myself because it was just me and the rain, and the rain wouldn't talk back to me; it would simply agree and continue to fall.

I think it is vital for the human soul to withstand the elements, live through them, walk in them, experience them, and survive them. There seems to be strength and growth in experience individually when you walk through the elements of weather and meet them head-on, where they are.

For this reason, I have never carried an umbrella or taken dry shelter from one. I want to be out in it, live in it, experience it, feel it; I want it to build the armor of my soul thicker so that I will be up for withstanding future storms.

Being from North Dakota offers a distinct element advantage in life. In that state, you experience the extremes of heat, cold, rain, and wind. After living there, you can live and thrive anywhere.

People think of the North as the coldest place in the United States. They believe that we wear gloves and jackets year-round, but they have never experienced a 100-degree week with 98 percent humidity. All they hear about are the minus-thirty-degree winter days with fifty-below wind chills and snow piled as high as your roof. That is a part of the experience as well, but just a small part.

The fact is, when you live there, you drive right through the elements, you work in them, play in them, embrace them. In short, you survive them and feel stronger in the human condition because of it.

There is a sense of accomplishment after deer hunting in thirty-below-zero and sitting around a campfire talking about the day. What isn't said but is felt is, "We are strong, we are resilient, we can withstand anything."

I miss those days, that cold, that heat, that wind that makes the wheat fields dance across the prairie. There I am strong, there I am uplifted, there I am free to run into the eye of storms and come out on the other side unscathed and better for it.

New York City, NY | 2018

Life in the Mind

The mind is a wonderful and fascinating thing. To know that we have a Rolodex in our brain that can collate, file, and record every circumstance and experience that we have gone through is both an amazing gift and an eternal tormentor at the same time.

When we encounter circumstances in life that challenge and hurt, we perseverate, these experiences within our mind and memory for a time. In doing so, we torture our current existence and limit our existence daily for a time.

In short, we are there, but we are not there. We are both present and absent, hearing, but not listening, living, yet dying to self for a time. The movies are horrors, and the reviews are endless and played back continuously for a time, if we allow.

In these times, if one takes the time to consciously think about and go to the file of good memories and experiences and attempts to align them side by side with the bad and push play, eventually, the good will win out. The days will come back into focus, life will resume as it always has, and hope and faith will once again rule.

Whenever I have had a good experience in life, I try to compartmentalize that in its own file cabinet, separate from the other. Here in this cabinet, life truly exists, comforts, and renews. Here, life is as it should be, a wonderful adventure with us as wandering, optimistic tourists.

Jost Van Dyke, BVI | 2020

The Soul of Summer

It's not a season, it's another one of God's gifts. The sun, the air, the smells, it's a tapestry from the divine for the masses.

Sand between your toes as you walk through white foam waves toward nowhere, yet everywhere.

The warmth of the sun breathes new life into skin cells hardened from the seasons before, and the colors remain the same. It's different, it's a touch from the creator, a fingerprint of His own placement on our skin.

It's shoes that have one sole and three strands that carry you wherever you choose to go. It's freedom, it's a beauty to be taken in.

The sun shines brighter, and the night turns darker. If you're lucky, a blanket of stars will light the way and nourish your soul in the stillness of the black.

Fires burn on beaches, raising flames to the skies to try and touch the hand that gave this setting this time of nourishment for the soul.

Music plays on sand and stone alike. Voices carry further in this time. Joyous anthems rise.

It's a feel-good state, a place where we are allowed to enjoy the humanness of being as we tame waves crossing waters of a blue hue.

All are welcome to partake, the sun freely gives, and the waters alike. It's our gift from The Giver. We're allowed.

To lay out and be nothing but still for a time to accept the rays that provide comfort and color the same.

Music sounds different in this season, over coals of fire and ale. Food falls differently on the palate from a grill or a sand smoker.

We feel alive in this time, we feel welcomed to this party thrown by the maker for us.

The sand, which he placed grain over grain that we walk through, cleanses the soul with each step.

Sounds carry, the ocean speaks. We listen and partake of nature's concert of waves and wind.

When I go to the ocean, I open the doors and listen. I need it to talk to me, to calm me to sleep. The patio remains open for the concert.

The power of that force builds me and helps me see how big and vast my God is. With a stroke of his finger, he commands the waves that now speak to me.

If you could bottle it, you could sell it and a king's ransom would be paid, but it's free, a gift to wash the worries of the day, year, past away.

Kenny sings of the islands and these same waters. I, too, inhabit that place; those people are my friends as well. They are now known but prefer to be unknown.

One island is different. The spirit of the people seems to float those masses of earth, keep them upright and lush with green in the hills.

Wherever the summer takes you, across a lake, highway, fields of gold, the ocean, or canyons of green, remember and be thankful for the free gift.

It was meant for your soul.

St. John, USVI | 2022

Me and Mountains

Mountains aren't just topographical structures for beauty to be viewed through our lens of life.

Mountains are in front of us, where we meet challenges in the mirror and when we step out into the roar of the world. It's up to us to conquer and silence them.

We were born and called to move them, navigate them, traverse them. It's a calling for the called.

The faith of a mustard seed is all that is needed to see them move, it is written.

I've climbed them, icy-covered, snow-encrusted, one step or corner to injury or death, no guard rails.

I need mountains. I think we all do. One step to life or death.

Think about the mountains in your life, what they look like, feel like, and alert your senses to.

When you're in the mountains, the smells are different, you're aware that you aren't the only inhabitant, you are aware of everything around you.

The trail and the bush ahead are the mystery. The overlooks are the gift for the gamble. The payoff for the paid.

They awaken a spirit in me, good and bad. Evil and Godly. One step from bridges on fire and the next footprint. Safe passage for the spirit and soul.

That's what mountains do. They appeal to the human spirit. Something about them awakens the lion in us and the lamb.

We choose to climb and conquer or stand in awe and look. The latter never gets ahead, only lets the mountain win.

I don't lose. Mountains will never win. They will be put in their place.

It's up to me and the mustard seed to ensure they are.

Ouray, CO | Ride West 2025

You Know

When she arrives, you feel more, and when she leaves, you feel less ... you know.

When the sun isn't as bright and the night is not so serene ... you know.

When the house is just a structure and not a home without her ... you know.

When a tropical island is just a rock and not a paradise in her absence ... you know.

When a Harley is just two wheels and not a sanctuary, traveling the countryside ... you know.

When a plane is just an aluminum tube and not a comfort ... you know.

When mountains, rivers, hillsides, and valleys are just the topography and not a beautiful canvas ... you know.

When a game is just four quarters and not an experience together ... you know.

When a kitchen is just full of appliances and not a work of art ... you know.

When a heart slows down when she departs, then speeds up when she is present again ... you know.

You know that you are more with her in your life and so much less without her ... you know.

When Proverbs 31 becomes real in the flesh in front of you ... you know.

You know you found the love of your life, and knowing that makes all the difference.

Pensacola, FL | 2024

Home

When people talk about wanting to go "home," it is not so much the physical space of the house as much as it is the idea of what that place means to them.

In my memories, home was a place of thought, and open idea sharing. It was a comfortable existence that included love and discipline, but mostly love, and always thought. There, my confidence was built, my life was started, the stones of my personal foundation were laid.

In this idea, I smell supper cooking, I hear my sisters talking, and my father coming through the front door to greet my mother. Instruments were played, voices were raised, and thousands of pages of books were turned. The downstairs was my domain, my restaurant, my entertainment room, my library.

In my mind, I'm always going home. I wear the coordinates on my skin, although my body hasn't followed lately. I am there in thought and reflection, and that is what sustains me and provides comfort when needed.

So I guess I would disagree with those who say, "You can't ever go home." I go there daily, and that makes all the difference.

Amsterdam, Netherlands | 2024

Hidden from View

What happens when the weather in your life never seems to change? The sun stays hidden for years, the rain doesn't stop, and the clouds never part. Where do you go, and what do you hold on to?

The thought that I have is that we have to believe in something. We have to hope that there is someone or something greater than us that will see us through, and provide a raft when the water is high, or shelter when the hurricane sounds outside the door of our existence. For me, that is God, the something and someone that I fall into the arms of.

I think it is funny how you hear of coincidences in life that aren't really coincidences at all, but are designed. For many years now, I have believed that we live a life of no coincidences, but rather we are a part of a wonderful and perfect plan that, through faith, only we can follow and stay present.

It is easy to doubt, and easy to make excuses, but in doing so, you rob yourself of the one thing that life foundationally is built upon: faith.

Faith that says we are, in and of ourselves, not strong enough to function alone, that we need help, guidance, and direction.

Faith that stands as a guardian from ourselves and our choices as being the end, or seeming like it is the end, and we are left with nothing but hopelessness.

Faith that sees a crack in the clouds, a letting up of the rain, and a confidence that the sun will shine again, and we will bask in its radiant light.

If the world can be created in a day, and the stars placed one by one, we can trust that we are in a safe harbor with the author of life.

Seaside, FL | 30A Ride 2013

We Are Followed

Ever feel like someone is chasing you? I mean, from the moment you wake up till the moment you go to sleep, and every time frame in between. Every thought, circumstance, choice, event, and every aspect of your daily life, someone is following you and chasing you down.

I am not saying this with a schizophrenic tone; that is not the thought; the thought is actually faith-based and proven. I believe each and every one of us is chased, and interestingly enough, by the author of the world. Think about that statement, and allow your brain to detonate and explode inside your head at the thought.

The ONE who places the stars in the sky "one by one," who breathed and the oceans were created in all their glory and massive power, the ONE who parted the Red Sea for humans to witness, told a guy to build an Ark in a drought, turned water to wine, defeated armies of thousands with a few, and died for us when he was found to be perfect, but WE didn't see it that way.

Yeah, that guy, he never sleeps. He embodies the modern-day mantra LIVE STRONG, and he cares enough about us, even when we spend most of our lives not caring enough about ourselves or others to merit that love or chase.

So, what does the ONE who chases us look like? Does he appear in conversations, circumstances, or coincidences? Is HE visible in the eyes of a child, or a mother's time? Is he in awe of our daily lives and persistent enough to chase us even when we aren't worthy of being caught?

The fact is, I don't know the answer to the above questions, and the longer I live, I am thankful that I don't have to. Because I am thankful HE does, I am thankful for a plan that's not my own, that leads to roads unseen on the Gantt chart of my mind and life.

No, I don't know, but HE does, and I am glad HE is in control, 'cause his thoughts are higher than mine, his ways are perfect, and his timing is impeccable. He is the friend who always "shows up."

Not knowing, I will still search in the daily goings on in my life for the one who is following me, 'cause I want that glimpse of perfection. I want to be found worthy of being chased.

I will look to have conversations with a mind greater than mine, and a love I will never understand nor deserve.

I will live the adventure and make stops where I need to, looking behind to see if, indeed, HE is visible, knowing He is back there somewhere ... watching, waiting, and loving ... in spite of who I am.

Thanks, God, for seeing me as worthy of your time, energy, and pursuit.

Pangkor Island, Malaysia | 2000

Your Cowboy

When you grow up in a family like I did, you look toward the future. It looks and sounds amazing in the mind's eye; the view through that lens is clear, unobstructed, and void of any clutter or obstacle.

In that view, you see a family of your own—kids, horses, dogs, family friends, vacations, a home church, and someone standing beside you, wandering your life and following your interests and your passions as you do the same for theirs. People say you marry your "best friend," and that may be true. I say we are all looking for our "Biggest fan."

My father is a simple, brilliant, strong, accomplished man. He is also an honest, hardworking, crack shot, build-it-yourself, help the neighbor bring the crop in, ass in the saddle, hand on the horn, cowboy.

As I wander through life, people often comment on my talents in every area of my life. They come from this man and my mother, but he taught me what a real man looks like, acts like, and lives like.

One of the greatest things my father taught me was how to treat a woman, your woman. This never took place in a conversation; there wasn't a watershed moment in time when we spoke in detail about this subject. He just lived it and let me watch. I was the fortunate onlooker to a man's life who showed up, who got it, who did it right.

In my father's home office, there was a plaque that hung. This plaque was of no grand flair, the horse in the drawing was not C.W. Russelesque, but the message branded my soul and still speaks to my heart as I look for her: "If a man has enough horse sense to treat his wife like a thoroughbred, she will never grow into an old nag."

Simple enough ... odd ... quirky, some might say, but after witnessing forty years of my parents' marriage, I know it to be true. I have seen it acted out in front of me my entire life by this man.

I read a lot, and I love quotes, I love independent thoughts, and I love to learn. For all that I have read, this simple, odd, quirky quote is like poets' words are to some. To me, it says more than what is written between the lines, over the lines, and under the lines; it says this, "Honey, I am your biggest fan. I will be in the first row cheering for your life."

It says that you will be taken care of; I will be the guardian of your heart. I will embrace you and your interests. Your passions will be my passions, your life will be my life, and your existence will make mine worth all the more.

I will be a front-row witness to your wonderful life, and you to mine. Wherever you desire to go in life, and whatever you experience and choose to pursue, count me in. We will navigate the waters of life together, and you will always be safe through storms. In me, you will always find a safe harbor, and the lighthouse will be my heart.

I will show up, and there will never be a time for me to worry about you 'cause I know that I will always be there, and should circumstance or chance make that difficult, time will be all that separates how soon I come to you in your time of need.

I will love you and hug you with open arms to allow you the freedom to be who God designed you to be, but in those open arms, you will never fall. I will cast away fear and eliminate doubt; I will keep the wolves of life a safe distance from the fire of our camp.

I will be your cowboy.

Although tomorrow is never assured, and the future we look toward together is a clouded mystery waiting to be ridden through, I will ride confidently anyway, I will clear the trail, I will assure safe passage, and I will bring you through whatever it is that we encounter.

I will ride into fear and the unseen confidently, so you can find comfort. Yes, I will be your cowboy.

Billings, MT | 2012

What Surrounds Us

I crossed states the other night (Oklahoma and Kansas) that most people would call wastelands. To the casual observer, there isn't much there; the scenery is as unique as the people who inhabit the land and call it home.

Being the product of a farm boy, a cowboy, and a professor has given me this perspective on life that most ignore or neglect to see. There is beauty in every state, in every area of our country, and in every experience, and in life, you just have to take time to find it.

I have sat in the finest restaurants in the world, and some of the greasiest spoon cafes you could find, sat in the swank booths of the W's of the world, and the sawdust-covered floors of a honky tonk. The Crown tastes the same, and I like and appreciate both equally.

I have seen the Alps of Europe, and the wheat fields dance in the wind of my North Dakota home, and I see God's hand moving across both. ...

I have conducted meetings in skyscrapers with mahogany conference tables and designer chairs, and conducted meetings in machine shops on a metal table fashioned for bending steel into form.

I have sipped coffee in a Times Square coffee house, and got my own Styrofoam cup, and sat with my late grandfather talking to the farmers at the elevator about their crops, and I cherish both, but the latter more.

Sitting on the shores of Pangkor in Malaysia and my ass in the sand of area lakes has the same, yet different, flavor.

I have sung on the stages of Nashville and in a bar where I was one of three in the room, but I sang anyway.

I have ridden in the finest cars, and I have driven one that I had to push down a hill to jump-start.

Sitting in custom-made designer deck chairs is the same to me as sitting in a deer stand on two-by-fours nailed to a tree for a temporary but meaningful time of solitude in the woods.

I have fished with a stick and twine, courtesy of a dead branch and whatever was available, for anything in the water, and I have crossed the Kachemak Bay of Alaska in a half-million-dollar boat and caught halibut as big as most people.

I have trampled across corn fields, sloughs, and sunflower fields in search of game on the farmlands of home, and the Alaskan tundra holds my footprint as well as I stalked caribou and moose on a guided hunt most would call the hunt of a lifetime.

I have rolled across the country, coast to coast, on my Harley-Davidson and covered that same expanse of land from 50,000 feet.

I share all of that, and there is much more to say this ... everything ... every place ... every time ... and most people you come across hold meaning. None is better or worse than the other; all are unique in experience and form. Perspective grants one this look, as does a curiosity to learn and live life out loud and with purpose.

I am often asked. "What is your favorite place that you have visited?" My response is always the same. Each place, each state, each country, each continent, each island, each town, each city, has their own beauty. It is up to you to find it.

The flyover state of Kansas looks like a checkerboard of Joseph's coat of many colors from the air. This state also annually produces the most wheat in the nation, and it's where the upper class and those who would be called the lower, even homeless, get their bread.

Oklahoma is a topographical conundrum of brush prairie and rolling hills. It is also where the suits of Wall Street are fortunate enough get the finest beef flown into Sparks and Brooklyn's Peter Luger Steak House to eat (both of which I have sat and partaken of their bill of fare), and, in some of their minds, change the world with their intellectual thoughts over a meal and a glass of merlot.

Each needs the other; it's up to all to understand this.

To be continued.

Miami, FL | 2019

Today I Watched Surfers

We all have heard the phrase "Waves of life." Today I viewed with my eyes personally, not through any filters, what that means.

I watched surfers today off the coast of Lima, Peru. From the start, I noticed many parallels between this sport and life. Instantly, I aligned with why this sect of the population is so passionate about this taming of an untamable force.

When they swim out from shore, they are forced to drive through, roll over, or duck and dive incoming waves to get to the breakers that will provide the best ride.

Some roll over and do not stop their progress, others force them to duck and dive underwater and be driven back for a time, then they paddle on.

All this to reach a destination that they see; it gives them the best opportunity to be successful on a ride back toward shore to turn around and do it again.

Some are successful when they time their mount and ride for two breakers or so, others get up and fall down after the wave has slowed, while still others get wiped out immediately.

The longer I watched, the more I came to the realization that I wasn't just watching surfers, I was watching the navigational course of life. Trial and error, the ability to catch another wave, live to fight another time. The perspective to see that the waves never stop coming, and they don't ask questions, just provide a powerful challenge.

On the waters and through the waves, I saw this ...

Choices, decisions, good relationships, poisonous ones, triumphs, great victories, and failures. Beauty, ugliness, deception, unexpected findings, the courage to move on and forward, or decide to quit. Long rides, short rides, rough waters, and calm seas, the ability to choose, and a chance to be fooled. Security, trust, chance, trials, the possibility of being destroyed quickly, or over time. Accomplishment and failure, fortitude and helplessness, courage and meekness, and winners, losers, and quitters.

Yes, today I watched surfers and my life, in the form of waves and the human spirit, fighting and challenging the great waters.

Lima, Peru | Miraflores District 2015

Change on the Rocks

The glasses are lined up on the bar pad. They have been dug in the tub for ice cubes, liquor spills over them, and they are filled, served, and consumed. Beer cans are cracked and opened, trays are set to serve, feet walk to tables, and hands transfer over the liquid thought of the moment ... and God is there.

Patrons line up, standing room only, profanities are echoed, eyes are set, some wander, others stare into space, belly up, grab chairs to fill a table, stand by a pool table, a jukebox, an entrance ... and God is there.

There are no secrets when people partake of the poison, *"in vino veritas"* (in wine, there is truth), and nare a truer word has ever been spoken. Doubts, questions, fears, thoughts, secrets, joys, pains, heartbreak, love, lost love, triumphs, defeats, the conquerors and the conquered in life gravitate to this place ... and God is there.

Some people would think it odd for God to be in a place such as this—a bar. Bars have a bad image for the most part, not on their own merit, but the consensus of the masses.

One needs only to look at scripture to understand where a living God would work, and it wouldn't just be within the brick walls of a church, a mission, a temple, a synagogue, or a parsonage. WWJB (where would JESUS be)? I say a bar, an alley, a lake, a road, a concert, a baseball field, a football field, a soccer field, a hockey rink, a park, a meeting room, or a balcony.

Think about this: we spend at most one day a week in church on average. We spend six days in the real world in all of these other places. Where do you think God would be? I would like to think He'd be in all of these other places and then He joins us on Sunday to celebrate and renew our thoughts and minds for the six days we face again.

Ever had that thought or ever allowed the thought to absorb in your mind's eye that no matter how far you fall in life, where you go, what you do, who you do it with, how you fail, how you fall, where that takes you, when you fall to the bottom, look in the mirror, stand in the shower, fall on your knees, cry about it all, struggle to stand, have a fear to speak, to take another step, because you feel unworthy, be considered a fool or a failure, then to realize there is an unconditional hand underneath your life that catches you and quiets it all. This hand controls it all—your life, your hopes, dreams, doubts, fears, questions, answers, failures, successes, addictions, sins, and your gifts. We always seem to forget about our gifts, it seems. I know I do.

I know God, for I have seen Him in the unlikeliest of lonely places in life. I have seen Him in bars, cabs, airports, coffee shops, ball games, homes, golf courses, hunting fields, sports fields, and places of vocation.

God is seen there because He inhabits our lives, our daily lives. No matter where it takes us, He chases us down.

Think about that and allow that thought to detonate in your skull and blow your mind. The God who created the heavens and the earth knows how many hairs are on your head, sees you in your current place in life, knows you, loves you, cherishes and wants the best for you, and chases you and millions like and unlike you.

Change doesn't occur in set places, change occurs where God chooses to inhabit. As for me, I most recently have seen a God chase me to a place and put people in my life where there was a choice to make, and there were changed lives in front of me. The ministered become the ministers, and the beauty of that is evidence of a living God. Neat, or on the rocks, shaken, or stirred, in a can, or in a glass, everyone has their preferences here, and God has His angels placed as well.

It doesn't matter where you find yourself. What matters is when you see God there, do you choose to drop it all and follow where He leads? Could be a conversation, or it could be a tear or a story. Could be change right in front of you, on the rocks, or a shot ... with a living God chaser.

Boise, ID | 2013

To Be Significant

My dad is a significant man. He shows up, he listens, he cares, he loves, his time is never his, he is always there for others. In short, he matters. He had a profound and significant effect on my life under his watch, care, and guidance, and now, his shadow of legacy in family and his example of time deposits in others are ever before me.

I love the man, and not a day passes that I do not think of him or ask myself in situations what he would do, or how he would react.

A family man of forty years, a man who cared about his son and two daughters enough to spend his weekends with us and his wife.

Looking back, young is a sweet thing and a venomous trek as well. I regret some of the things I said to him. I understand now the term "wisdom years," and "because he said so" matters to me, and shaped me in countless ways foreign to me then.

I guess he loved me in spite of myself. He cared no matter what I said, and he knew that his time and guidance were seeds that needed time to nurture and grow. He understood that storms would come, and the sprout would be challenged and challenge him, yet he had confidence in who he was and what he said, and I do, too. In short, time spent with my dad shaped me as a man and as a nomad in this world.

My dad made me feel like I mattered, I had gifts and talents, I was good at things I did, and I could accomplish great things. He and my mother encouraged and taught me to have confidence and to work hard at anything I set out to do, and my God-given gifts would come out.

Together, they laid a foundation of Godly confidence in who we were and, more importantly, *whose* we were. They mattered, and they knew it would matter when life didn't request their son's permission to change course.

At times in my life, I have felt significant to others. I thought that my time mattered, that my investment in their lives was deposits with lifelong returns, that trust and transparency with one another were present.

When you feel like you are needed, that you make a difference, and that you are planting seeds daily, weekly, and monthly in others that you choose to have close, you really feel like you matter. So much so that at times you get lost in what you are doing and who you are doing it for, and you begin to feel deserving, you begin to feel unduly important, and a sort of arrogant cloud in who you think you are hangs over you.

Have you ever felt that way? Have you ever found that really you are only important if you are important in the eyes of those you are busy doing for? I have, and that cloud that followed began to let loose, and then the storms came.

That's when life became the instructor, and I was deserving of nothing but questions and disbelief in who I perceived myself to be in the eyes of others at times.

In sales, there is a phrase that says, "Value added is only really value added if the customer perceives it to be." All the executives and management sitting in meetings discussing how great a product is, why it matters, and why it will matter to make a consumer purchase it really doesn't matter if it hits the market and the customer doesn't see the benefit to them. This is not only true for business, but for relationships and life.

I am thankful I had such wonderful teachers as my parents, who taught me what true DVA, documented value advantage, is.

"It's not the critic who counts."

People think you ride because you have a death wish. I ride because I have a life wish, and I embrace it through the wind we all one day will ride through as fate takes its course. I test it on the open road, and if I should become a part of it, I know I was not a cold nor timid soul who feared my destiny.

Louisville, KY | 2020

The Birds of Brooklyn

There are birds in Brooklyn.

I know because I was awakened by their morning melody.

Amidst the concrete and the vertical building structures, they too have a home.

Above the noise of the city waking up, they are heard as they move from perch to perch.

This is their home too. Not just a place for the masses to inhabit or survive.

Sitting high above the sirens and the sounds of a city coming to life in the a.m., they watch and sing.

They see the hustle and the struggle, they observe the traffic of a monster coming to life to be fed.

This monster that feeds millions feeds them too from the same corner Italian bakeries. Houses them as well in the foliage amidst the jungle of concrete as some would call it.

But amidst that jungle, there is life and there are birds.

There are flowers that bloom in front of structures built hundreds of years ago. Fashioned by hands that created this place.

Between the two a bridge separates providing another perch for them as well. Pedestrians and cars allowed and they too.

Another skyline view location to look over the cities and sing. Sing to the giants that awake and become the monsters of commerce and trade for another day.

Soon the streets will fill, and the sounds of another day will drown out their melody.

Neighborhood coffee houses will open their doors, pouring caffeine for the morning jump needed to start this machine for another day.

The pace will quicken throughout the day. Horns will be heard from all streets, voices raised out windows with fingers.

The crescendo will be reached much later here. The afternoon will see establishments filled with the caretakers of these monsters sharing their stories of the day over ale.

Subways running beneath will carry them from burrow to burrow.

Taxis, bridges, and sidewalks ... the same.

It takes them all to nourish these beasts for a day, to turn the gears that propel these two engines of the world.

Who are these beings, they wonder, who worry and stress about the day and walk with a violent pace?

We are the birds of Brooklyn, look how we are clothed, sheltered, and fed.

Surely they are more important than us.

Brooklyn, NY | Bedford Stuyvesant District 2025

3002

That is where she was, in the window. Putting her life and career on hold to watch me hit a ball across the street, catch a pass, fight, walk to the rink in minus thirty with fifty-below wind chills, skates on my stick, through thigh-deep snow.

This was Fargo. Those dashes in front of the numbers are real.

A scholarly professor cared enough about us and a home to wait for us to bloom, grow, and have a foundation.

Before she ascended in her career, as she was destined to do, she was there in that light through the window over the sink. Watching everything, praying, and wishing the same.

I gave, and still give, those prayers a run, wishes too. But ...

She was and is always there.

She was the cornerstone of that house with my father at 3002.

The bread was always fresh. I never understood the menu, few would, 'cause she wasn't from this place, she was global, but you wouldn't know.

If you know what kohlrabi is, you are ahead of me, not her.

She was always the smartest in the room, but never made anyone feel that way. They knew, I didn't.

Her words were strong but held meaning. Her silence did as well.

The way she read to us told us she cared, told us that time was all that mattered. Learning had meaning.

Reading was encouraged, manners were taught, and the piano was too.

The Bible was read, God was ever present, Jesus wasn't just a frame on our wall, and verses were committed to memory.

It was home; she made it that way.

It was where I was told, in between hockey practice and piano lessons, "Get in the car; you're getting a job."

The manager at Hornbacher's grocery was Pat. She introduced us. I filled out an unnecessary application, and it was done.

I began bagging groceries and stocking shelves at fourteen.

We were allowed to fail, to learn, to grow, to work, and to understand life there.

The kitchen table was the place to settle differences and discuss life and dreams.

It is where I learned to "Run to the Roar" when I told her there was a boy who wanted to fight.

That phrase wasn't for that fight—it was for life. It is now in ink on my arm.

3002 coordinates are the same in black, next to the Fargo Theatre, and next to the lion with the cross.

All was committed to memory at 3002. It was the intention of a professor, of a mom.

My sleeve of home, that now is a part of me, she might as well have held the pen and needled into my flesh herself.

She hates tattoos; she didn't know they were for her. She does now.

It is home; it is where, no matter how far I have traveled across the world, I always go back to.

When I am on two wheels across this country, taking it in, home is ever present in my mind.

It is where bikes were scattered across the lawn, and the flowers she planted bloomed alongside us, the hedge was trimmed, and the grass was always cut.

The backyard was where the Vikings played the Steelers, we fell out of trees, and we learned to get bruised and cut and get back up.

The place was and is special; she intended for it to be and made it so.

It wasn't just numbers on a mailbox, not just GPS coordinates to a structure, it was home.

It will always be.

I miss it. I miss her presence in my life's window. I talk about her daily in my life, and she doesn't know.

It's important that she does.

She knows now.

Hamburg, Germany | 2024

About the Author

L. Seth Burchill

L. Seth Burchill, originally from Fargo, North Dakota, has spent twenty-five years in the industrial aftermarket as a global sales specialist, a career that has taken him across the United States and around the world. He now lives in Denton, Texas, with his daughter. *Riding Lions* is his debut book.

"For my part, I travel not to go anywhere, but to go.
I travel for travel's sake: The great affair is to move."
— Robert Louis Stevenson

Thank You for Reading My Book!
DOWNLOAD YOUR FREE GIFTS

Just to say thanks for buying and reading my book,
I would like to connect with you.
Scan here to visit my website and get social media links.
Scan the QR Code:

I appreciate your interest in my book and value your feedback, as it helps me improve future versions of this book. I would appreciate it if you could leave your invaluable review on Amazon.com.
Run to the Roar ... Thank you!

www.ingramcontent.com/pod-product-compliance
Lightning Source LLC
LaVergne TN
LVHW011422080426
835512LV00005B/217